SRA
OPEN COURT READING

The Game Pieces

SRA

A Division of The McGraw·Hill Companies

Columbus, Ohio

www.sra4kids.com

SRA/McGraw-Hill

A Division of The **McGraw·Hill** Companies

Send all inquiries to:
SRA/McGraw-Hill
8787 Orion Place
Columbus, OH 43240-4027

ISBN 0-07-569753-X
   3 4 5 6 7 8 9 DBH 05 04 03 02

A hole is in the game box.
The game pieces fell out.
The pieces fell in this field.

This piece is a chief's hat.
It was by the tree.
Jeff spotted it.

This piece is a shield.
It was by the rock.
Mollie the dog helped find this piece.

This piece is a race car.
Nellie picked it up.
Nellie is my niece.

The cup was in the middle of the field.
I believe Walt stepped on it.

It was so much fun to get the pieces.
We will make a new game.
We can call it "Hide the Pieces in the Field."